T0161119

Ross's

Thoughtful Discoveries

Michael Ross

Ross's

Thoughtful Discoveries

Michael Ross

Rare Bird • Los Angeles, Calif.

This is a Genuine Rare Bird Book

A Rare Bird Book | Rare Bird Books
453 South Spring Street, Suite 302
Los Angeles, CA 90013
rarebirdbooks.com

FIRST HARDCOVER EDITION

Set in Minion
Printed in the United States
Distributed worldwide by Publishers Group West

Publisher's Cataloging-in-Publication data

Names: Ross, Michael, author.
Title: Ross's thoughtful discoveries : quotes from literature on reality, thinking, reasoning,
and contemplation / Michael Ross.
Series: Ross's Quotations
Description: First Hardcover Edition | A Genuine Vireo Book | New York, NY;
Los Angeles, CA: Rare Bird Books, 2018.
Identifiers: ISBN 9781945572678
Subjects: LCSH Books and reading—Quotations, maxims, etc. | Quotations, English. |
BISAC REFERENCE / Quotations
Classification: LCC PN165 .R67 2018 | DDC 808.88/2—dc23

*To all my family, friends, teachers,
professors, shipmates, partners, mentors,
colleagues, and students who gave me
"reality checks" by making me think,
reason, and even contemplate*

Introduction

In *Ross's Novel Discoveries* and *Ross's Timely Discoveries*, I offered some personal information to support my bona fides in selecting topics and quotes to share with readers. In each case, I cited my reading experience and my personal relation to the topics. In the interest of avoiding repetition (and promoting sales of the first two volumes), I will not repeat most of the information in the introductions to them.

Although there are many, including many among readers of this and my previous books, who have read more and better books than I have, I have concentrated my reading on literary fiction that has stood, or seems to have a strong likelihood of standing, the test of time (putting aside for the moment some simply fun reading).

I have read, and continue to read, classic, modern, and contemporary novels; short stories; and plays. Although most of these are by US authors, there are many from other countries. Readers will certainly find holes in my reading choices—that is, excellent writers I have missed—and consider some of my sources of selected quotations undeserving of their attention. Nonetheless, one of my aims in these collections is to introduce readers to authors and works they may not have encountered.

The publication in the last two years of *Ross's Novel Discoveries* and *Ross's Timely Discoveries* has affected my reading in a number of ways, some for the better and others for the worse. One positive change is that I have endeavored to read a wider variety of authors, including some that are new to me but have reputations as strong contributors to the literary canon. I should confess here that another reason for my diversifying the authors whom I read is the passing within the past few years of several authors from whom I collected numerous quotes, for example: Peter Matthiessen, Günter Grass, Ivan Doig, E. L. Doctorow, William Trevor, and Jim Harrison. Some quotes from new writers may be included here and in subsequent volumes. I am also more conscious of searching for quotable passages in the works I read. This may distract me from a greater appreciation of the work of literature as a whole. I continue to wean myself from my prior compulsion to finish each book I start. The number of books I have set aside is increasing, perhaps in part because I am not finding quotable pieces. I am also reading less nonfiction than I did previously.

It seems more difficult this time for me to suggest a special relationship with the topics in this volume than it was for the prior two. I doubt that I have a much closer connection to reality than my readers. My life experiences and reading may have made me more astute than some and fuller of illusions than others. The recurrence of themes from both sources has given me some confidence that my selection of quotes will be thought-provoking, interesting, and sometimes humorous. In any case, I believe these topics are very worthy of exploration and consideration.

My career practicing mergers and acquisitions law at a large law firm and as general counsel of a large corporation prescribed large doses of thinking, reasoning, and analysis in several ways. One was mastering relevant facts, including identifying misleading evidence and knowing what I did not know. Another was, of course, understanding and applying the law to the facts, often in situations in which the application was uncertain. Yet another was an evaluation of the audience for my advice or negotiating position, for example, a senior partner, outside client, corporate boss, or opposing party. I confess that my practice left little time for contemplation. My post-practice teaching career (at two US and foreign law schools and a private Croatian university) afforded much greater opportunities for reflection, not only upon the subject matter of my practical seminars and lessons learned from my practice but also upon my role in teaching soon-to-be young professionals. The process of selecting topics and quotes for my books has created more opportunities for contemplation.

As with the first two volumes, there is substantial overlap among the topics in this one. One might easily rearrange the main topics, subtopics, and quotations. I have tried to think carefully and reasonably about the order. I hope readers will not let any disagreements interfere with their enjoyment of the book.

The more I read literature and, unavoidably, the older I get, the more I am persuaded of the value of quotations. We encounter them in many areas, such as formal education, religion, politics, and comedy. They can inform, educate, awaken, enlighten, and amuse us, sometimes all at once. We may be influenced, even molded, consciously or subconsciously, by quotes we remember and requote to others. They also provide us with effective ammunition for our discourse with others.

Reality

What is reality? I consulted my old *Random House Webster's Unabridged Dictionary* (2001) for some answers. It offers a few affirmative ideas, such as: "What is true, existing or occurring in fact, actual, genuine, authentic, and sincere." As well as some antonyms it is not, such as: ostensible, nominal, apparent, imaginary, ideal, fictitious, counterfeit, artificial, imitation, and feigned. Is any of that dispositive, or are there more questions?

Is there only one, or more than one, reality? Do we perceive reality mainly internally, or mostly through external stimuli? What internal and external difficulties and obstacles do we encounter in our efforts to perceive reality? What is the role of knowledge as it relates to reality?

Do we create our own realities, and, if so, why, how, and what are the consequences? These questions are frequently explored by philosophers, psychologists, and psychiatrists, so it may come as no surprise that they are the subject of substantial consideration by authors of literary fiction and their characters.

Is there an "objective correlative," as Eliot might have put it? One of my favorite authors in one of my all-time favorite books begins by suggesting a simple, straightforward answer, but then hedges a bit:

《》

Verification is the only scientific criterion of reality. That does not mean that there may not be realities that are unverifiable.

John Fowles, The Magus

The quote below, from one of my favorite contemporary authors, asserts rather forcefully that there is "really" only one reality and uses an unusual adjective to describe the alternative:

《》

...and with the coming light I feel a certainty: that there is, despite our wild imaginings, only one life. The ghostly others, no matter how real they seem, no matter how badly we need them, are phantoms. The one life we're left with is sufficient to fill and refill our imperfect hearts with joy, and then to shatter them. And it never, ever lets up.

Richard Russo, *Bridge of Sighs*

I found a contrary suggestion from one
of my favorite contemporary authors that
there are, in a way, two realities:

《》

*The real and the imagined are one. Thoughts
are real, even thoughts of unreal things.*

Paul Auster, Man in the Dark

If there were only one reality, perhaps
it could be made up of the "real"
and "unreal":

«»

*This was the great truth of life, that fact and
fiction were always merging, interchanging.*

Graham Swift, *Mothering Sunday*

An Irish-born British author, who was well-known for his successful short stories, has his character discover that one of these possible realities was less than reliable:

«»

When you imagined, you were often wrong.

William Trevor, "Of the Cloth"
in *The Hill Bachelors*

A popular, prolific American author has his character create from a routine management tool, a novel idea for a "new reality." As a list maker myself, I can appreciate the proposition:

«»

Of course the lists of things were also things. An item on a list might generate a whole new list. He knew if he wasn't careful he'd get mired in a theory of lists and lose sight of the things that needed doing. There was a pleasure in lists, taut and clean. Making the list, crossing off the items as you complete the tasks. It was a small whole contentment, a way of working toward a new reality.

Don DeLillo, Mao II

Notwithstanding these alternative
realities, a previously quoted author
in a different work rejects, seemingly
categorically, unreal realities, but is
he hedging?

«»

*No one wants to be part of a fiction, and
even less so if that fiction is real.*

Paul Auster, "Ghosts"
in *The New York Trilogy*

What are the sources of our perceptions of reality? Are they principally internal or external? A well-respected author and expatriate who spent most of his writing career in Morocco raises the question quite persuasively:

«»

What strange things happen in the mind of man. No matter what went on outside, the mind forged ahead, manufacturing its own adventures for itself, and who was to know where reality was, inside or out?

Paul Bowles, *The Spider's House*

One of America's best known contemporary authors makes the argument that reality is to be found inside us:

«»

Reality didn't exist "out there." It began to be real only when the soul found its underlying truth. In generalities there was no coherence—none. The generality-mind, the habit of mind that governed the world had no force of coherence, it was dissociative.

Philip Roth, *American Pastoral*

Another popular, contemporary
American author suggests that our
internal perceptions vary during our
waking hours, using an interesting choice
of adjective:

«»

*You know are who you are when you wake
up more than when you go to bed when your
filigree abilities are at their highest.*

Jim Harrison, "I Forgot to Go to Spain"
in *The Beast God Forgot to Invent*

Here is an author who complains that our internal perceptions may be skewed to our disadvantage:

«»

Gullibility and innocence, unmitigated by even a smidgen of healthy cynicism, might not represent everything that was wrong with America, but it was a grotesque combination.

Richard Russo, *Bridge of Sighs*

Along somewhat similar lines, this Nobel Prize–winning, post-war German author advocates one attitude and warns against another:

«»

Remaining skeptical is better than turning cynical.

Günter Grass, Too Far Afield

As this highly regarded author, who set his novels in the Northwest, points out, there are limits to one's ability to perceive reality. He uses an excellent, quotable metaphor, one that might stick with us:

《》

Not even a contortionist...could see all sides of himself at once.

Ivan Doig, *Prairie Nocturne*

An internationally known Czech-
born French author offers a transition
for some people from internal
to external perceptions:

《》

*People who see their lives as a shipwreck set
out to hunt down the guilty parties.*

　　　　　Milan Kundera, Ignorance

The next step is to explore a few external sources of our perceptions. This one focuses on a likely source:

«»

After all, if children don't make you see things differently—first bringing them into the world and then watching them go out into it—then God help you.

Ethan Canin, *America, America*

One of the authors who captured my
attention as a much younger reader uses
an interesting combination of simile
and metaphor to illustrate outside
sources of perceptions:

«›»

There were Japanese TV sets all over the prison. They were like portholes on an ocean liner. The passengers were in a state of suspended animation until the big ship got where it was going. But anytime they wanted, the passengers could look through a porthole and see the real world out there.

Life was like an ocean liner to a lot of people who weren't in prison, too, of course. And their TV sets were portholes through which they could look while doing nothing, to see all the World was doing with no help from them.

Kurt Vonnegut, Hocus Pocus

This quote, from one of my favorite
contemporary authors, introduces
an example of an external perception
of reality:

«»

*Imminent peril has difficulty staying
imminent if it doesn't at least show a
glimpse of itself.*

Ivan Doig, *The Whistling Season*

A similar notion about the effects of external perception comes from a Canadian-born New Zealand author in her historical novel set in her home country:

《》

It often happens that when a soul under duress is required to attend to a separate difficulty, one that does not concern him in the least, then this second problem works upon the first as a kind of salve.

Eleanor Catton, *The Luminaries*

One of the possible conclusions to be drawn from the quotes above is that there may often be a combination of internal and external sources of our perceptions of reality:

«»

It was funny, even if so many of the things she heard every day were in her head, she always thought at first, before things got sorted out, that were outside her head.

Robert Penn Warren,
Meet Me in the Green Glen

A famous Canadian writer of excellent trilogies, among other novels, suggests a practical compromise:

«»

We make a deal between what we can comprehend intellectually and what we are in the world as we encounter it. Only geniuses and people with a kink try to escape, and even the geniuses often live by a thoroughly bourgeois morality. Why? Because it simplifies all the unessential things. One can't always be improvising and seeing every triviality afresh.

Robertson Davies, *The Rebel Angels*

As the following quotations will reflect, there are numerous difficulties and obstacles that interfere with our perception of reality. They come in all sorts of sizes, shapes, and forms. We will start with some that are internal in nature:

A prolific nineteenth- and twentieth-century British writer asserts that problem is with our capacities:

«»

"We, none of us, had a clear vision of reality; nobody perhaps would ever do more than approach reality. What we perceived was just that much of reality that got through to us, through our very defective powers of interpretation."

H. G. Wells, *Christina Alberta's Father*

According to an attorney/author whose
novels and stories I always enjoy, our
defects apply with particular force
to self-examination:

«»

We are all fallible, especially about ourselves.

Louis Auchincloss,
"Priestess and Acolyte"
in *Tales of Yesteryear*

A Nobel Prize–winning British writer of Indian descent, who set some of his novels in his home country, Trinidad, makes a very similar point, one that probably has international application:

《》

It's always easy to see the other man's strangeness.... We can't see our own strangeness.

V. S. Naipaul, *Magic Seeds*

Another source of interference
is identified by another of my
favorite authors:

«»

*I decided not to doubt it as it seems to me
that doubt is often an example of self-pity, a
kind of whining about existence.*

Jim Harrison,
"The Man Who Gave Up His Name"
in *Legends of the Fall*

One of my favorite British authors adds another internal condition that distracts our attention from reality:

«»

How was it possible for anyone to plan his life or regard the future with anything but apprehension?

Graham Greene, *The Confidential Agent*

The source of many of our difficulties may
be our feelings or sentiments, which can
get in the way:

«»

*Funny about feelings, they seem to come
and go in a flash yet outlast metal.*

John Updike, *Rabbit Is Rich*

It should, perhaps, come as no surprise
that this author expresses strong criticism
for feelings' effects. Is he exaggerating?

«»

Feelings can be life's biggest problem.
Feelings can play the most terrible tricks.

Philip Roth, Indignation

A well-known American writer of the Western US condemns (if it is not too strong a word) sentiments:

«»

"In the end we all come to be cured of our sentiments. Those whom life does not cure death will. The world is quite ruthless in selecting between the dream and the reality, even where we will not. Between the wish and the thing the world lies waiting."

Cormac McCarthy, All the Pretty Horses

A previously quoted British author, in the same novel, suggests that part of our problems may be in describing reality:

«»

A word was not a thing, no. A thing was not a word. But somehow the two—things—became inseparable. Was everything a great fabrication? Words were like an invisible skin, enwrapping the world and giving it reality. Yet you could not say the world would not be there, would not be real if you took away the words.

Graham Swift,
Mothering Sunday: A Romance

Dreams, fantasies, and illusions
are allegedly also to blame for
obscuring reality:

«»

*How easily, in the absence of children, the
whole experience of life became abstracted,
a pattern of words and daydreams.*

Peter Matthiessen,
At Play in the Fields of the Lord

Is this often humorous author correct that it is really "everybody?"

«»

Everybody had dreams of doing something else.

Jules Feiffer,
Harry, The Rat With Women

So are fantasies to be avoided or merely kept in reserve or context? And can they become, in some sense, real?

«»

I like to avoid fantasies so that it's more of a surprise when it happens.

Jim Harrison,
"The Man Who Gave Up His Name"
in *Legends of the Fall*

A writer acclaimed for his historical literary fiction offers an example of an apparently recurring illusion:

«»

You may think you are living in modern times, here and now, but that is the necessary illusion of every age.

E. L. Doctorow,
The Waterworks

This quote captures what I think is a common illusion, at least one about which the older generation often comments:

《》

When you're young and think you'll live forever, it's easy to think life means nothing.

Thomas McGuane, Keep the Change

There may, however, be some benefits to these dreams and illusions; they may, somehow, lead us to reality:

«»

All misconceptions are themselves data which have the minimal truth of existing in at least one mind. Truth…is not something static, a mountain-top that statements approximate like successive assaults of frostbitten climbers. Rather, truth is consistently being formed from the solidification of illusions.

John Updike, Of the Farm

This author, often quoted in my books, offers a very concise description of his perceived benefits of dreams:

《》

Only our dreams gave life any coherence.

Jim Harrison, *The Road Home*

A very prolific American author, whose
political views were often controversial,
argues against taking away our illusions:

«»

*Some people, maybe most people, can only
live by illusion, and the cruelest thing in the
world is to deprive them of those illusions....*

Gore Vidal, *Two Sisters*

We need to consider some external and natural difficulties. If the subject is other people, they may not be what they seem or purport to be:

«»

The lovers of the simple were too inevitably complex.

Wallace Stegner, *Second Growth*

Here is another thought, and a very succinct one, about the difficulties of knowing people from, in my opinion, one of the best contemporary American writers of literary fiction:

«»

Anyone could be anything, for an hour.

Richard Powers,
The Echo Maker

One of my favorite authors, of whose
books I think I have read all but the
most recent, notes another element
of confusion:

«»

*People change and places change and what
once was will never be again.*

T. C. Boyle, "Rastrow's Island"
in *Tooth and Claw*

One of the very few writers of mysteries whom I read (and I think I have read all of them) comments on a similar issue in one of his very early and less well-known books:

«»

Urgent equals ephemeral, and ephemeral equals unimportant.

John le Carré, *A Murder of Quality*

Another complicating factor, according to this writer, is the lack of absolutes; he uses a creative analogy of laws of physics to make his point:

«»

Because well-being and need are purely relative concepts. There is no such thing as poverty in itself, suffering in itself, unhappiness in itself. All is relative... Absolute motion is unobservable. Only the relative motion between two objects has meaning.

Alan Lightman, *Reunion*

Randomness, according to an author well-known for his popular novel that was made into a successful movie, presents a significant obstacle. His metaphor is quite descriptive:

«»

There seemed no plausible connection between cause and effect, or ends and means. History was a trash bag of random coincidences torn open in a wind.... Results attained were unrelated to objectives envisioned.

Joseph Heller, Good as Gold

We should consider another view, albeit a bit of a pessimistic one, of a fundamental stumbling block:

《》

You and I, each in our own way, are looking for something that isn't really there. We're looking for connections that may or may not be there and, finally, if we are lucky, we are looking to find a pattern in the shape of events. Well, the more I study this cruel and crazy century, the more I am haunted—not convinced, *mind you, but anyway deeply haunted—by the prospect that there may not be any pattern. That the only pattern, the one constant in a world of accidents and variables, is our wish for one, our hopeless, feckless desire to find one.*

George Garrett,
*The King of Babylon Shall
Not Come Against You*

An American writer of a few very perceptive and humorous novels uses an interesting metaphor to describe how our efforts to discover reality are led astray. It is a bit long, but worth the effort:

«»

We modern human beings are looking at life, trying to make some sense of it, observing a "reality" that often seems to be unfolding in a foreign tongue—only we've all been issued the wrong librettos. For a test, we're given the Bible. Or the Talmud or the Koran. We're given TIME *magazine, and* Readers Digest, *daily papers, and the six o'clock news; we're given school books, sitcoms, and revisionist histories; we're given psychological counseling, cults, workshops, advertisements, sales pitches, and authoritative pronouncements by pundits, sold-out scientists, political activists, and heads of state. Unfortunately, none of these translations bears more than a faint resemblance to what is transpiring in the true theater of existence, and most of them are dangerously misleading. We're attempting to comprehend the spiraling intricacies of a magnificently complex tragicomedy with librettos that describe barroom melodramas or kindergarten skits. And when's the last time you heard anybody bitch about it to the management?*

Tom Robbins,
Half Asleep in Frog Pajamas

Before turning to another question, here is a creative, but more concise, exposé of the unreliable evidence of reality:

«»

It was curious and pathetic; everybody behaved nobly and made a lot of money. It was as if some code of faith and morality had been lost for centuries, and the world was trying to reconstruct it from the unreliable evidence of folk memories and subconscious desires—and perhaps some hieroglyphics on stone.

Graham Greene, The Confidential Agent

Implicit in the quotes and commentary above is the question of the role of knowledge in ascertaining reality. An American Nobel Prize–winning author explores, in one of his lesser-known works, the concept of knowledge:

«»

"It's a strange thing this knowing. It is nothing but an awareness of details. There are long-visioned minds and short-visioned. I've never been able to see things that are close to me. For instance, I am much more aware of the Parthenon than of my own house over there."

John Steinbeck, The Pastures of Heaven

This well-known British writer weighs in about what is necessary in order to gain knowledge, introducing a bit of irony:

«»

You don't know the real things until you've sampled the false.

Graham Swift, Tomorrow

We may need some wise counsel about the pace of obtaining knowledge and its potential consequences:

《》

For knowledge comes slowly, and when it comes, it is often a great personal expense.

Paul Auster, "Ghosts"
in *The New York Trilogy*

As with our perceptions, there are obstacles to our achieving knowledge, as this quote very succinctly describes:

《》

"The only thing I know for sure is you can never be too misinformed."

Richard Powers,
Generosity, an Enhancement

This author's character is frustrated by his apparent inability to gain knowledge:

«»

Nothing was ever entirely as it seemed, he found himself thinking, and he didn't know why he did.

William Trevor, "Of the Cloth"
in *The Hill Bachelors*

Perhaps we are incapable of knowing, as this quotation suggests, with a hint of the cruelty involved:

«»

Really how life goes on is a secret, you only know your memory, and it makes its own time. The real time leads you along and you never know when it happens, the best that can be has come and gone.

E. L. Doctorow,
Welcome to Hard Times

One of America's very highly esteemed
authors reminds us that knowledge is one
thing, but knowledge of the things we
should know is another:

«»

*We knew all kinds of things but not the
ones we needed most to know. Modern
achievements...jets, skyscrapers, high
technology, were a tremendous drain
on intelligence, more particularly on
powers of judgment and most of all on
private judgment.*

Saul Bellow, *The Dean's December*

A famous British playwright's well-known character, Higgins, wonders about our knowledge of ourselves and asks a couple of probing questions:

《》

"Besides, do any of us understand what we are doing? If we did, would we ever do it?"

George Bernard Shaw, *Pygmalion*

So what happens if we do not know something—that is, does it change reality?

«»

I wonder whether if a person does not know something has happened it is the same as if nothing had happened.

Graham Swift, "Seraglio"
in *Learning to Swim*

Knowing is one thing, but what about the consequences of not knowing?

«»

In fact the blow hurts less than the threat—the blow's momentary, the threat you worry about. But the true pain, at least to me, is when you don't know what you have to know.

Bernard Malamud, "Talking Horse"
in *Stories of Bernard Malamud*

If we could figure out reality and find we do not like it, we could create our own. The number and quality of the quotes below suggest that this is not an uncommon strategy. If there were a spectrum or range of these measures, using intoxicants or pleasurable undertakings and pastimes might be at one end. If used in moderation, what would be the harm?

《》

God knows it's hard enough for a man to adapt himself to circumstances; why should you deprive him of his little assistants in the difficult task? Wine, for example, learning, cigars and conversation, art, cooking, religion for those that like it, sport, love, humanitarianism, hashish and all the rest. Every man has his own recipe for facilitating the process of adaptation. Why shouldn't he be allowed to indulge his dope in peace?

Aldous Huxley, Those Barren Leaves

The use of one device or another might be quite temporary, and if the subterfuge does not last long, would it be so bad?

«»

Anyone could be anything, for an hour.

Richard Powers,
The Echo Maker

As with many things, there may
be a "slippery slope." That is, once
we start inventing some things, we
might go on to create more and more
significant deceptions:

«»

*People who are self-glamorized invent their
peculiar significances as they go along.…
Until they knit together a dazzling fantasy.
They turn themselves into something like
glorious dragonflies and whiz through an
atmosphere of perfect unreality. Then they
write essays, poems, whole books about
each other.…*

Saul Bellow, *Ravelstein*

Resorting to one's own version of reality
could be the result of an inability to cope
with contradictions and inconsistencies
that we perceive in reality:

«»

*Such entanglements of truth and falsity—of
good and evil, God and the Devil—Michael
dwelt upon in the hermitage he had created,
while the seasons changed and the days of
his life were one by one extinguished.*

William Trevor, "The Virgin's Gift"
in *The Hill Bachelors*

This commentary about self-created reality points out a benefit and a potential harm:

《》

"When a person is lucky enough to live inside a story, to live in an imaginary world, the pains of this world disappear. For as long as the story goes on, reality no longer exists."

Paul Auster, *The Brooklyn Follies*

The author here suggests that most of
us engage, to some degree or another, in
making our own reality:

«◇»

*For surely most people live more in their
own fiction than in their own fact.*

Louis Auchincloss, *Diary of a Yuppie*

We might suppose that if our created reality is somehow "real" then the role might fit well. But is that what this quote means?

«◊»

We go through our lives playing ourselves.

Richard Powers,
The Time of Our Singing

This English novelist, poet, and critic, suggests that, perhaps, if we do not stray too far, the benefits will outweigh the downsides. This seems to be refinement on the thought expressed in the prior quote:

«»

So we act: we choose a part not too incongruous with our age and station and play it out to the best of our ability and energy. We can't keep it up all the time, but it's there when we need it....

Kingsley Amis, *Russian Hide and Seek*

A previously quoted author's character seems to be very liberal about allowing us to engage in some creativity when it comes to our reality:

《》

"And people have a right, I suppose, if they can afford it, to purchase their own brand of reality."

Louis Auchincloss, "The Lotos Eaters"
in *Tales of Yesteryear*

This one questions whether there may be limits to our protectiveness of our own reality, using a somewhat extreme case:

«»

Does the madman know he is mad? Or are the madmen those who insist on convincing him of his unreason in order to safeguard their own idea of reality?

Carlos Ruiz Zafón,
The Shadow of the Wind

The question might then arise about what
reality to try to create, and what might
be others' reactions to it. We can count
on this British playwright's insight and
caustic commentary:

«»

*"If you pretend to be good, the world takes
you very seriously. If you pretend to be bad,
it doesn't. Such is the astounding stupidity
of optimism."*

Oscar Wilde, *Lady Windemere's Fan*

At some point, the creativity and role-playing becomes deceitful:

《》

A lie, after all, is only another way of affirming the desirable. A live lie is better than a dead truth, and there is no ultimate wall that the creative individual cannot breach through deceit.

William Kennedy, Roscoe

Nonetheless, this highly regarded British playwright, novelist, and short-story writer condemns lies to a particular audience:

《》

If it is necessary sometimes to lie to others it is always despicable to lie to oneself.

W. Somerset Maugham,
The Painted Veil

And the consequences of engaging in downright deceit, wherever the line is crossed, may be disastrous:

«»

For when those first days come along it is easy for a man to deceive himself and begin to believe that maybe he shall live forever. And once a man believes that, even ever so briefly, why it seems to follow that any kind of mischief is allowed and likely to succeed.

George Garrett,
The Succession: A Novel of Elizabeth and James

The same author in another of his novels makes the point again, perhaps a little more strongly:

«»

How easily we become the victims of our own masks, costumes, and disguises!

George Garrett, Double Vision

Whether the consequences of creating our own realities are beneficial or detrimental, we may end up with little choice about what to do with what we have created:

«»

"If you've pretended this long, the only decent thing you can do is to keep right on pretending as long as you live no matter what happens."

Joseph Mitchell, "Joe Gould's Secret"
in *Up in the Old Hotel*

A common theme about creating our own version of reality is that we do it out of our concern for what others think of us:

《》

Her trouble was that she saw herself just as she was and at the same time saw the different image that she managed at times to create in the eyes of others. She saw herself as doomed to wear a mask, and were not masks in the end almost invariably detected? Life's trophies went to the self-deceived or to those who were capable of deceiving with relish.

Louis Auchincloss,
The Lady of Situations

This prize-winning author describes
how we determine what role to play to
reconcile ourselves to others' expectations:

«»

*Life is like this—people playing their parts.
People try to sense what others expect of
them, they derive a picture of themselves
from the clues they pick up from others, and
then they are driven to oblige—sometimes
without even knowing it.*

John Hersey, The Conspiracy

Here is a somewhat complicated explanation, including quite an exercise in irony, of how some people perceive or fail to perceive the acts they put on for others:

In fact, those who most seem to be themselves appear to be people impersonating what they think they might like to be, believe they ought to be, or wish to be taken to be by whoever is setting standards. So in earnest are they that they don't even recognize that being in earnest is the act. For certain self-aware people, however, this is not possible: to imagine themselves being themselves, living their own real, authentic, or genuine life, has for them all the aspects of a hallucination.

Philip Roth, The Counterlife

I feel compelled to end this section with a quote from the same author in the same book because this quote summarizes the effect of everyone's creating fictional selves based upon the expectations of others:

《》

The treacherous imagination is everybody's maker—we are all the invention of each other, everybody a conjuration conjuring up everyone else. We are all each other's authors.

Philip Roth, The Counterlife

Thinking,

Reasoning,

and

Contemplation

Thinking

We might have started this book with these three topics because they are usually necessary components of discerning reality. They are, however, also relevant to other topics. The questions about thinking, reasoning, and contemplation have some themes in common. Many address the benefits and values and the downsides, especially of excesses. Others identify the limits or the difficulties and obstacles encountered with these endeavors. Do we think about thinking, and if so, what do we think about it? This seems a bit circular, but there may be some value in spending our thinking time wisely.

A reasonable, albeit not the only rational, starting point may be an encouragement to think. In this case it comes, with a little sarcasm, from a teacher to his students:

《》

Read the questions carefully. Take your time. Try to think a little. You may find it a novel and interesting experience.

George Garrett, Poison Pen

Should we question how we think? Do you agree with this interesting proposition?

«»

We think in images, not in words....

Vladimir Nabokov,
Look at the Harlequins!

We probably all agree there are some benefits to engaging in this exercise. This quote comes from a favorite author who died too young:

《》

But say it was true that devotion to some mighty realm of thought meant escape from the vanity of hope and striving. What switch turned on the gift for caring about the possibly beautiful structure of the universe?

...

In the practice of philosophy, as in the practice of law, or novel-writing, or almost anything else, one gained things inexpressible to anyone not in the practice; no harm that what you gained would die with you, to be regained, inexpressibly by someone else.

John Gardner, *Mickelsson's Ghosts*

This author, who has an astute perception and a clever way with words, offers his assessment of importance of thinking:

《》

For curiosity, especially intellectual inquisitiveness, is what separates the truly alive from those who are merely going through the motions.

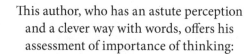 Tom Robbins, *Villa Incognito*

Who can argue against thinking? It appears that a character in this novel by one of America's finest Southern authors can:

«»

"It's always thinking makes things bad. If you just don't remember nothing. Just don't wait for nothing. Just keep *now* in your head. A man can stand anything if it is only just that second. If a man just keeps *now* in his head, there ain't nothing else."

Robert Penn Warren,
Meet Me in the Green Glen

According to this perspective on our ability to think, there are some substantial impediments:

«»

As the social order goes haywire and the constraints of centuries are removed, and the seams of history open, as it were, walls come apart at the corners, bonds dissolve, and we are freed to think for ourselves—provided we can find the strength to make use of the opportunity—to escape through the gaps, not succumbing in lamentations but getting on top of the collapsed pile.

Saul Bellow, "Cousins"
in *Him with His Foot in
His Mouth and Other Stories*

Here is a fun simile for a perceived difficulty with thinking. Have you ever felt like this?

«»

Trying to think was like picking through a rubbish dump looking for nothing in particular.

Kingsley Amis, Stanley and the Women

So, perhaps, we generally, or at least sometimes, appreciate people who make us do it:

«»

Even at her worst she made you think, and that's worth something in a person.

Ivan Doig, *The Bartender's Tale*

According to this author of some controversial works, there is an allure of being able to settle into a time of thinking:

«»

For who would venture out into that gray miasma of perpetual smoke and fog that filled the streets if he might remain walled up with books, sipping black coffee, smoking black Russian cigarettes, thinking long, black, inky thoughts?

Edward Abbey,
"Manhattan Twilight, Hoboken Night"
in *The Serpents of Paradise*

According to my favorite Canadian author, some people may not be very competent with this endeavor. The simile he uses to describe the character's decision-making is very effective:

《◇》

To begin with, he had discovered, now that he was well into middle age, that he did not know how to think. Of course he could pursue a logical path when he had to, but in his personal affairs his mental processes were a muddle, and he arrived at important conclusions by default, or by some leap that had no resemblance to thought, or logic, or any of the characteristics of the first rate fictional criminal mind. He made his real decisions as a gifted cook makes soup: he threw into a pot anything likely that lay to hand, added seasonings and glasses of wine, and messed about until something delicious emerged. There was no recipe and the result could be foreseen only in the vaguest terms.

Robertson Davies, The Lyre of Orpheus

There are, of course, thoughts about what happened, but here is an example of thoughts about what, apparently, had not happened, or did not seem to happen:

«»

He thought to become again the child he never was.

Cormac McCarthy, *The Crossing*

One of my favorite authors offers us some thoughts on the downsides of thinking. Both of these are from the same novel:

«»

These times we live in give us foolish thoughts to think, dead categories of intellect and words that get us nowhere.

If he didn't pull himself together he'd suffer from random thoughts. Those were the worst—they ate you up.

Saul Bellow, *The Dean's December*

Despite these cautionary messages, we should end this section on a positive note, a call for more and better thinking:

«»

From the beginning of the twentieth century
Freud sent a loud wake-up call to mankind,
to become aware of what lay beneath the
surface of the mind, and to mend its ways
accordingly. And mankind, as always
through history, has halfheard the call of the
prophet, half-understood what he says, and
vulgarized and cheapened whatever of his
teaching may come its way. But something
has been achieved. A few holes have been
thrust through the wall of human stupidity
and incomprehension.

Robertson Davies, *The Cunning Man*

It is one thing to think but quite another to engage in reasoning, especially cogent, logical, rational, reasonable reasoning. It seems to come naturally to some but less naturally to others. What, if anything, can be done to encourage more and better reasoning? It is not my doing, but the quotes I have collected seem to focus predominantly on difficulties with reasoning.

It seems appropriate to begin with a very concise expression of one of our important obstacles:

«»

The mind has a mind of its own.

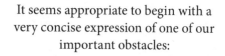 Paul Auster, *Man in the Dark*

Here is a rather humorous admission by a character of the source of his difficulty reasoning under the circumstances:

«»

Exactly what I was going to do remained a little unclear. You have to remember that I'd hoisted a few and my mind, while it had flashes of brilliance, was not at its analytical best.

Robert Plunket,
My Search for Warren Harding

A favorite author from when I was
much younger succinctly offers a
serious limitation on the efficacy of his
character's reasoning:

《》

*The flaw in his reasoning, of course, was
that exemplary conduct presumes someone
to benefit from the example.*

John Barth, Letters

It seems that there may be circumstances or situations in which the rational and the logical do not work well. Have you experienced any of these?

«»

And there're happenings in this life that simply don't lend themselves to rational interpretation. To look at them logically can be to look at them wrongly. Logic can distort as well as clarify.

Tom Robbins,
*Fierce Invalids Home
From Hot Climates*

A famous and prolific British playwright's character, Statue, wonders if there may not sometimes be too much of an otherwise good thing:

«»

"But I am quite content with brain enough to know that I'm enjoying myself. I don't want to understand why. In fact, I'd rather not. My experience is that one's pleasures don't bear thinking about."

George Bernard Shaw,
Man and Superman

A pitfall is often how easy it is for us to convince ourselves of what we thought or felt in the first place:

«»

It is surprising how persuasive you can be when talking into your own ear.

Ivan Doig, *Work Song*

This prize-winning American novelist and playwright gives us an apt description, with a vivid metaphor, of the effort it may take to reason something to a proper conclusion:

《》

But the most exhausting of all our adventures is that journey down the long corridors of the mind to the last halls where belief is enthroned.

Thornton Wilder, *The Woman of Andros*

Although reasoning may be difficult, or fraught with interference, we might hark back to advice from a classic:

«»

And let this ever be lead to thy feet, to make thee move slow, like a weary man; both to the yea and nay thou seest not; for he is right low down amongst the fools who maketh affirmation or negation without distinction between case and case; wherefore it chanceth many times swift-formed opinion leaneth the wrong way, and then conceit bindeth the intellect.

Dante Alighieri, The Divine Comedy

Contemplation

Contemplation involves more than thinking and may include some reasoning or something more. Whatever it includes, it seems to have some depth. These quotes may make us wonder if we should spend more or less time in contemplation. In either case, we might ask about the benefits and detriments of doing so. In order to end on a positive note, our first quotes will explore some of the problems with contemplation and related considerations. They will be followed by more positive ideas.

A recurring issue is about having too much of an otherwise good thing. Here is one complaint with a simile that should resonate with those who have had committee experience:

《》

The problem with the contemplative life was that there was no end to contemplation, no fixed time limit after which thought had to be transformed into action. Contemplation was like sitting on a committee that seldom made recommendations and was ignored when it did, a committee that lacked even the authority to disband.

Richard Russo, *Empire Falls*

If our contemplation is about difficulties, issues, vexations, or the like, a downside is not being able to escape:

«»

Problems, once you conceive of them as problems, never let you alone.... All occasions inform against you if you're problem-haunted.

Saul Bellow, *The Dean's December*

The same sentiment is expressed in this observation, which includes a little advice:

«»

A man can worry himself ancient. Step them off, the days, that's what we need do.

Ivan Doig, Sea Runners

At some point, the excess can apparently be debilitating:

«»

He was desperate because the constant companionship of unanswered questions was affecting his nerves and suggesting that it was the absolute final and daily condition of living.

Thomas McGuane, *Keep the Change*

Here is a similar notion, with an interesting turn of a phrase:

《》

I told myself that I could soon start to relish the state of being alone…only to find, as usual, that being alone meant that I was stuck with myself, with the outside and inside of my body, with memories and anticipations and present feelings, with that indefinable sphere of being that is the sum of these and yet something beyond them, and with the assorted uneasiness of the whole. Two's company, which is bad enough in all conscience, but one's a crowd.

Kingsley Amis, *The Green Man*

Overdoing it might even affect our perception of time and sound:

«»

How silently the world revolved, when one was brooding, and alone.

                                Eleanor Catton, The Luminaries

Our engagement in contemplation may set
us apart in meaningful ways from others:

«»

No, it's the not the fools who turn mystics. It takes a certain amount of intelligence and imagination to realize the extraordinary queerness and mysteriousness of the world in which we live. The fools, the innumerable fools, take it all for granted, skate about cheerfully on the surface and never think of inquiring what's underneath. They're content with appearances...call them realities and proceed to abuse any one who takes an interest in what lies underneath these superficial symbols, as a romantic imbecile.

Aldous Huxley, Those Barren Leaves

Perhaps, an appropriate way to finish
with negative consequences is to offer a
humorous characterization:

《》

*"Philosophers are good at parties but not for
cleaning up after."*

Lorrie Moore, *A Gate at the Stairs*

A very creative British writer, philosopher,
and novelist identifies a natural obstacle
to contemplation:

«»

*Habit was a stifling, warm blanket that
threatened you with suffocation and
lulled the mind into a state of perpetual
nagging dissatisfaction. Habit meant the
inability to escape from yourself, to change
and develop....*

Colin Wilson, The Desert

This Polish-British author, regarded by some as one of the best novelists to write in the English language, finds benefits in contemplation even if it yields a rather pessimistic outlook:

«»

I felt in my heart that the further one ventures the better one understands how everything in our life is common, short, and empty; that it is in seeking the unknown in our sensations that we discover how mediocre are our attempts and how soon defeated!

Joseph Conrad, "A Smile of Fortune"
in *Twixt Land and Sea*

This contemporary American author
offers a low-key assessment of the value of
some contemplation:

«»

*In the solitary life there was a tendency to
collect moments that might otherwise blur
into the rough jostle, the swing of a body
through busy streets and rooms.*

Don DeLillo, Mao II

It seems like this character has engaged in some contemplation before collecting his thoughts about contemplation:

《》

I knew that what was wrong with my life and work was that I was so busy accumulating and organizing facts and experiences that I had failed to perceive that only in the contemplation of mystery was revelation possible; only in confronting the incomprehensible and arcane could there be any synthesis.... I had become a creature of rote and method at a time when only intuitions culled from an anarchic faith in unlikely gods could offer me an answer. How could I ever come to know anything if I didn't know what I didn't know?

William Kennedy, Quinn's Book

Here is a recommendation in favor of contemplation and advice for how to do it:

«»

Those who chafe at the tameness and sameness of office life, who pine for a little excitement to diversify the quotidian routine, should experiment with this little recipe of mine and bring the water-shoot into the counting house. It is quite simple. All you have to do is to pause for a moment in your work and ask yourself: Why am I doing this? What is it all for? Did I come into the world, supplied with a soul which may very likely be immortal, for the sole purpose of sitting every day at this desk? Ask yourself these questions thoughtfully, seriously. Reflect even for a moment on their significance—and I can guarantee that, firmly seated though you may be in your hard or your padded chair, you will feel at once that the void has opened beneath you, that you are sliding headlong, fast and faster, into nothingness.

Aldous Huxley, *Those Barren Leaves*

A highly regarded Southern author makes a strong case for contemplation's role in life:

《》

The search is what anyone would undertake if he were not sunk in the everydayness of his own life.... To become aware of the possibility of the search is to be onto something. Not to be onto something is to be in despair.

Walker Percy, The Moviegoer

We may not always like or welcome the
results of our contemplation:

«»

Introspection is a rude visitor.

Ivan Doig, *Work Song*

Nonetheless, we would do well to take seriously this admonition from a writer whose use of the vernacular is very effective:

«»

It's about the time that we start viewing the world as something other than a whoop-de-doo playground, we start to experience personally how threatening it can be, how cruel and unjust. At the very moment when we become, for the first time, both introspective and socially conscious, we receive the bad news that the world, by and large, doesn't give a rat's ass....

Tom Robbins,
*Fierce Invalids Home
From Hot Climates*

For some characters and people,
contemplation is invaluable:

«»

*Solitude. I have known the pure joy of being
alone in contemplation.*

John Hersey, *The Conspiracy*

A fitting finale to this section should be a call for balance:

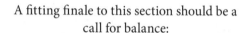

It was necessary to live and then to justify, to balance the contemplated and the true. It was necessary to experience life correctly but at the same time compose it into something acceptable.

Robert Stone, *Outerbridge Reach*

Afterthoughts

No matter how much time and effort we spend thinking about reality, reasoning about our connection or lack of connection to it, contemplating the consequences of our relationship with reality, we may still find many unanswered questions. We may still wonder what it is we really know and believe. This reminds me of a bumper sticker (or "snicker," as Paul Harvey used to call it) that read: *You don't need to believe everything you think.* Because we are busy and life is short, we might be wise to spend some time thinking about what it is we think about. None of these quandaries should suggest that the time and effort engaged in thinking, reasoning, and contemplation is not worthwhile. Even if we do not solve the mysteries of reality, our thoughts, reasoning, and contemplations of our lives and the lives of those near and far make us who we are.

I would like to express my deep appreciation for Tyson Cornell's enthusiastic support and creative ideas for this third volume of my quotations, and for the hard work by all of the staff at Rare Bird, including Alice Marsh-Elmer for the development and execution of the excellent design, inside and out, of the book; Hailie Johnson; Julia Callahan; Gregory Henry; and Jake Levens.

Thanks to Cara Lowe for the illustrations.